HIVESTRUCK

HIVESTRUCK

VINCENT TORO

PENGUIN POETS

PENGUIN BOOKS
An imprint of Penguin Random House LLC
penguinrandomhouse.com

LIBRARY OF CONGRESS CATALOGING-IN-PUBLICATION DATA
Names: Toro, Vincent, 1975– author.
Title: Hivestruck / Vincent Toro.
Other titles: Hivestruck (compilation)
Description: New York : Penguin Books, 2024. | Series: Penguin poets
Identifiers: LCCN 2023054925 (print) | LCCN 2023054926 (ebook) | ISBN
9780143137771 (paperback) | ISBN 9780593511886 (e-book)
Subjects: LCSH: Technology—Poetry. | LCGFT: Poetry.
Classification: LCC PS3620.O5878 H58 2024 (print) | LCC PS3620.O5878
(ebook) | DDC 811/.6—dc23/eng/20231201
LC record available at https://lccn.loc.gov/2023054925
LC ebook record available at https://lccn.loc.gov/2023054926

Printed in the United States of America
1st Printing

Set in Calluna
Designed by Jessica Shatan Heslin/Studio Shatan, Inc.

To Grisel, as always . . .
And to all the Brown Cyborgs everywhere . . .

Are we humans mere machines
to manufacture machines better than ourselves?

—Ernesto Cardenal

Contents

HIVESTRUCK

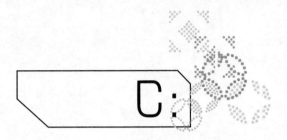

Because they love the pixel, not the hero.

—Hito Steyerl

iArs Poetica : MicroGodSchismSong

Robot pilgrim colonic. Illicit volt rot.

       Motor imp. Six-digit pinprick.

Sonic broom.   Scoop fool's gold from

       slipshod mind pod.   Pick locks

of COBOL roosts. Phototrophic bliss,

       phonic distortion. Tinfoil trolls

in Wi-Fi torpor. Oblong X   Box flips

       ribs into port prisons or sim

forts. Iris lit with Nook prisms. Whip two

       million gig pistil. Piston shift

from groin to droid rods. Zip witch or whiz

       kid. Proto-Snob incision. Toxic

pools of blown skin trips. Thin Fission

       of word from window. Mint

condition solipsism. Ion soot loops. Bitcoin

       cops kiss in biochip gridlock.

Nitric worm hollow.   Info mortis.

"such acceleration produces fusion."
—Octavio Paz

Uggs are so five minutes ago.
So, too, are Crocs. I threw out
my pair before anybody knew
they had been made, just
ninety-eight seconds

        after I bought them. Fresh is old,
        tu sabes? Like on fleek. Or
        scallywag and greaser. Like my abuela's
        Tinder profile. Yo, I can't get with

foxtail suits, the new neon space jumpers.
My foxtrot now buried in the basement
with my running man. My Charleston.

        No one uses those formats anymore,
        don't you know. They're mad outdated.

Like CDs. Or cassettes. Or live symphony orchestras.
Or Reason. Though all the really cool bands
are now releasing their albums on papyrus
sheet music. Those days which are these days

        my folks are hooked on WhatsApp,
        while mi sobrina says for her 11th birthday
        she just wants a daguerreotype machine
        and the chance to hike device-free
        this Sunday which is already last Monday.

I'm told realism is back and abstract
minimalism is better left as set pieces
in period films from a time no one seems
to remember. And besides, no one goes
to films anymore. But I hear the silent era
is fixing to make a spectacular comeback,
and cuneiform is about to cancel Moho.

Today human resources is scanning
job applications using an algorithm
that discards the résumés
of candidates older than
the age of fifteen. And those
fifteen-year-olds better
be able to prove that they have

        no experience and at least
        two million followers. Though
        HR says they are all for hiring
        anyone who's already been
        dead at least seventy years,
        but they have got to be willing
        to start in the mail

room. Pero I also heard mail
rooms are relics and fiber
optics are obsolete, that nano

        is the next old thing.
        My kid brother is already
        hooked. He asked
        for a candelabra
        and a windup music
        box for his sweet
        forty-third. What,

then, is the current trend? you ask. Stare
down that tunnel up ahead. In twenty
seconds you'll see a train that's
headed for the last century.

        Union busting last Friday
        becomes Matawan
        next Tuesday. The Bolshevik
        revolution and Bolivian

independence will be held up
as both errors of the past and triumphs
of the future. The French symbolists

are the future's hot-girl summer,
Nahmean? Nah, they're so passé.
Haven't we seen that done before
next Tuesday? Comic books are suddenly

        trends for the nursing
        home. What we'll say in a decade
        is already out of fashion.

It's like everyone is pining
to be the flavor of the millennium.
(But which one?) Trending items dissolve
into the ether faster than Hydrogen Sulfide.

        We're already bored with
        what hasn't happened yet.

Binge Watch

Caught the season (Hail) finale
of So you think (Hail) Ninja Idol
the Housewives of (Hail) Abbey
A young soldier was (the distracted)
baking when (the over) a spurned
lover informed him of his mother's
cancer Then a shot clock buzzed
(stimulated) The ball hovered
desperately like a caped (the cross)
wizard at zero hour (the under)
Soon a school hallway (nourished)
broke into song and (their allergy)
venomous creatures (to action)
ascended from sewers
(has calmed) while coworkers
cast aside etiquette to kiss
(the avalanche) Ten doors over
(Somatic) teen mothers are
castigated Emergency surgery
(Amused) is performed without
anesthesia The (the front) crew
(gate) hunts for the world's
weirdest sandwich A neighbor
(was left open) cracks wise A drug
deal (for us) goes awry Widows
bicker at the dead (to walk in)
gladiators bob (and rob) in spandex
across synthetic foam battlefields
News lands with (the starstruck)
a joke A bomb is defused mere
seconds before it was rigged to
detonate Wax sealant is sold
to (the desolate)
the nonplussed

A Brief History of My Screens

My first screen was large
                    enough to fit me inside
          its mandibles. Immobile, it weighed
                              as much as a baby rhino.
                It poked me with grainy
sculptures of showrooms
                    filled with domestic wares
                    begging me to guess
          how much they cost. How much?

          *

My second screen was smaller
                              though still unable
to migrate with me to untenable borders.
          The lines were sharper
                    like a spaghetti strainer where
          I tried to sneak my broken action
                              figures through. It always
refused to go dark when bed-
                    time came to arouse me.

          *

                    My next screen did not belong
to me or to any relatives. He was
          a stowaway in the front
                              room I shared with two
          flatmates (or maybe I was
          the stowaway). One of them could
                              always be seen trying
to wedge themselves into the tubes,
                    vying for space among
          the clicks, among the cliques
                    that this screen promised
                              would make us all beautiful.

*

My fourth screen was desperately lonely. We mostly
    kept it turned off because we
        were too busy falling in love,
        and besides,
    it had terrible reception.

*

        My fifth screen Gremlin-multiplied
    until there were more screens than rooms.
        They, too,
          despise sunlight, water.
   Devoted, they have learned to be a walk
   through Tokyo streets, a Pacific beach,
      or even an eagle's nest.
Fluorescent balm for analog chafing, my pores
     engorged by their lucent marvels
        until I became a twisted
   nematic hominid, living liquid crystal shroud.

*

   (So much time spent
        looking, looking, searching,
   hoping something . . . anything . . . was looking
        back.)

Panopticonfederacy

He longs to discover a nook of the couch
where no living thing might find him, a place
occupied by the swarm of jump-cut edits
where thin men launch themselves down traffic

storms with cardboard signs and fists full
of conviction. Each angle offers him pastiche
where the ungroomed dance to silent rhythms,
circling the local pharmacy with only their grimace

to protect them. Their need to press against
each other and urge neighbors to throw up their
arms bedevils him, or it makes him bitter, or
perhaps it makes him sanguine. Sanguinely bitter

to be told they demand a seat at the feast where
bloodstains become poker chips. Or so he is told.
He is told and so he tells. No need to cross-
check dispatches. Their willingness to act to cry

to sleep in littered ATM stations astounds him.
He can't imagine wanting anything so badly.
He can't imagine wanting. He can't imagine.
When the pepper spray is drawn and the crowd

becomes subsumed by SWAT shields and fire
hoses, his heart rate settles into the muted hum
of an electric fan. It's like something he's seen
on TV, this thing he's seeing on TV. He figures

they'll only get what they deserve. Or they'll
deserve what they get. They must be mad,
he figures, to want more than the crystal clear
picture they get on their phones. He remembers

dial-up, and answering machines made of magnetic
tape. He wonders what more could one need
than a freezer full of chopped meat. They're
spoiled rotten, he thinks. The machine reminds

him that his favorite reality program is about
to begin. *What was I just thinking?* he thinks.
His bowels clench. He reaches for the armrest.
Grunts. Wiggles between the seat cushions,

stares down the wire tapestry of ultraviolet
light that stares him down, tempting him to blink.

iDécimas

:

I am an icon. My profile
page when double-clicked updates you
on my status. One million views,
I've gone viral, less man than file,
I am a case of Tweets gone wild.
Text without context, discontent
content, my Skype is omniscient.
Mecha-molting, I'm the new breed.
For skin contact, there is no need.
With the right apps, I'm transcendent.

:

My news feed bleeds minced reflections

of protesters in the Ivory

Coast, in Saint Paul, rote eulogies

for the latest dead thespian,

smear ads for the next election.

I can fix it all by posting

on your wall. Can prove by boasting

on your thread that I'm a vanguard

in the movement. I wield a card

to appraise the bird now roasting.

:

Lodge this web until the face bloats.

Crack spines and decipher streams.

Splice pickup lines with scripture. Steam-

boats were once people. The new moats

are firewalls of misapplied quotes.

Generate culture from feedback

and distortion. Digimyth. Hack

mainframes and mind frames. Cellophane

self from serf. A legerdemain.

Cyborg hubris slyly bushwacked.

Vaporware (Beta Test)

thumb blister eyeshot   node fried and dehydrated
           cathode rays collated
and creeping into personal   life palette pixelated

hours meals spent   staff meetings vacated
           for high scores combing
for codes to secret levels   rewired dendrites reroute

old ghosts eradicate   baby boy's first steps
           capture enough gold rings
to upgrade weapons   to unlock levels

screen warp inoculation   fantasy finally waning
           warning virtual perfume
sprayed bow to   the socket the plug

days boosted into seconds   joypad titillations
           bowel breaks back
aches sun shunned   hunched over chipped

coffee tables through   beryllium and zinc
           pleasure fission astigmatic
arthritic aging without   growing without

traveling without   traversing within
           konami code stasis
pwned jebaited in   supramarginal gyrus

no easter egg no extra   lives to be earned
           no next level debuffed
maturated into infancy   cerebral cortex soldered

to motherboards   as voltage of avenue
                    brio outside freezes
reformats reboots vitiates   digits into entropy ellipses

St(r)atus Updates

Two cross-eyed mockingbirds play chess with dismantled satellites.
Like· Comment· Share· 30 seconds ago

A crosswalk made of hyperbole. A crossing guard wearing an xEMU.
Like· Comment· Share· 8 minutes ago

We are all victims of bad lighting.
Like· Comment· Share· 47 minutes ago

Corpses give birth in empty estuaries where clip chimps renew their smartphone contracts.
Like· Comment· Share· 3 hours ago

Nothing is an exact science. *Everything* is an art.
Like· Comment· Share· 8 hours ago

She is insomnia, ambitious to be narcoleptic.
Like· Comment· Share· 15 hours ago

The amputation was conducted with an opal feather duster.
Like· Comment· Share· 23 hours ago

It's all bars and beats and rhythms and measures and melodies and vamps and riffs and bridges and hooks and chords and choruses and keys and octaves and changes and harmonies and refrains and solos and
Like· Comment· Share· 1 day ago

Fences fleeing from ground. Ground pleading with sky.
Like· Comment· Share· 6 days ago

Delivered like a pancreas to the wrong ward.
Like· Comment· Share· 11 days ago

Daydreaming is sacred.
Like· Comment· Share· 20 days ago

"'Using single quotes within double quotes is a sign of impending insanity,' quoted Andrei Codrescu, quoting Nabokov."
Like· Comment· Share· 23 days ago

Halfway through the cocktail party I realized that I was the drink and not the straw.
Like· Comment· Share· 49 days ago

Was Han Shan the first tag banger?

Amplifiers propped up like black ziggurats.

The therapist's therapist prescribed him to catch the ferry across the river and get off halfway.

Bemused muses conspire on a fuzzy silver continent.

Incontinent, their consonants collaborate, fashioning innovative forgeries.

My head like a proscenium.

I had to bury an egg to prevent the dream from becoming reality

Kandinsky's ghost is permanently ineligible for a platinum Visa.

The New Testament was a suicide note!

Or a tattooed crocodile.

The Mir space station has been sent its third eviction notice.

To adore numbers but deplore mathematics.

Roll up the cities. Let the window explode into coalitions of burnt flowers . . .

He was trying to talk to himself, but he kept refusing to listen.

Who are we but condensed milk, cutups of cleaves of impressions left by retired ballerinas?

Harlequins iron their masks on beds of gold hyacinths.

Like · Comment · Share · 401 years ago

All Random All Mid!

Like · Comment · Share · 887 years ago

Only my frauds seem original, like dry land on a drowning man.

Like · Comment · Share · 1,111 years ago

Invisible lines replacing visible ones.

Like · Comment · Share · 2,286 years ago

A single purple

Like · Comment · Share · 10,000 years ago

Algorithmontuno : HechiZOMG

Every time you touch an app, you are basically just touching a metaphor, a conduit into an operating system linked to more metaphors layered on metaphors about the unfolding equations defining the data you see on the screen in front of you.
—Paul D. Miller, aka DJ Spooky That Subliminal Kid

An app to call your mother for you on
her birthday. An app to turn traffic
into a tulip garden. An app
for when your favorite sweater
                    is ready at the cleaners.
          An app that draws blood
moons onto the walls
          at the post office.
          An app that predicts when
                    a pineapple will ripen.
An app that shares
                    your wittiest anecdotes
with the nearest hogs. An app to kneel
          for you when your sister's
melanoma is malignant. An app
                    to agree with you when
the audience has fallen asleep. An app
for when your birthday bludgeons
                    you with dour questions.
An app to celebrate each time another
dishwasher gets fixed. An app that begs.
An app that listens even when
you are entirely incoherent.
An app to sell off your old
magazines and an app that
refashions dentures into colonnades
whenever the blows you struck
crawl through your intestines
                    clogging your best intentions.
An app that rots or riots
                    on command. An app that
          functions without a thumb

to guide it. An app to eliminate undesirable
                    scents. An app that shakes
the sand from your bathing suit
          while checking your father's
cholesterol. An app that goes home
                    with the wrong guy
          for you, so that you can
go home with the right one.

Bot Cento of Donna Haraway : Cyborgoddess Codexegesis

Blasphemy. Blasphemy. Blasphemy protects my cyborg

    of intimacy. Baroque of uncoupled reproduction. Chimera

        machine arguing a cosmos of mud and the vanguard.

    Science of upstart god mocking pain in Detroit. Number

worshippers making chips to transgress the monstrous.

    The color experience weaving alienation and illusions.

        Polyvocal failures, polymorphous labor in bionic role-

    play. Disassemble. Reassemble. A techno-digested body,

a cryptology of babies and baboons. Obscene de-skilling.

    A hunger militarizes the imagination. Hunting now done

        with cameras. Telematic citizenship in a simultaneity

    of breakdowns recodes the noise. Code pollution with no

original dream. The cyborg refuses to disappear on cue, scoffs,

    speaking with whales, and pilots planets. The body

        that is map. Not innocent, it hugs irony, pleasures

    machine it builds. Regenerates. Not birth. Lost limbs guide

us to the maze. Our fears reconstructed into transmogrified I.

Content Moderator's Lament

it's something more. no less. than trash. what i've viewed.

a dereliction of cubicle and the unfathomable macabre.

from this cavern. i sort through it all. flag each AVI

transgression for a substandard salary with no benefits.

there's the beheadings. the suicides. the unmentionables.

that i am paid to screen. things that can't be unseen.

boss told me. it was an important job. that i would be

the gatekeeper. the front line protecting community

standards. but what community? and what are

the standards? for this occupation there is no

employee manual. no professional development

seminars. to guide me. boss tells me not to take

a position on what i observe. my decisions must

be made solely. on what is legal. not what i consider

decent. i was hired to prevent lawsuits. not judge

people's ideas or practices. boss tells me. abuse

of children. of course. must go. but the swastikas

and leaked celebrity nudes. are fair game. engagement.

boss tells me. is worth more than dignity. every evening

i walk home along the same polluted river we once

were pressed to bathe and pray in. make my way

to a prefabricated apartment. i am able to call. my

own. find my way to the dinner table. to kiss my

spouse and children. while trying to scrub from my

pupils. the horrors i've spent eight hours monitoring.

my charge. to watch the worst of what this world uploads

to its servers. all so my children can one day live on

the side of the partition that pays people like me

to scald their retinas. so that a barrister in Manchester.

can enjoy their macchiato without geysers of snuff films

spurting from their consoles. staining their prim snouts.

iSestina : Guaguancóokies.exe

scroll ad scroll text pic scroll swipe ad text pic
ad ad swipe text send pic swipe pic scroll scroll
send swipe send ad ad ad pic text send text
scroll ad scroll ad scroll ad scroll ad scroll ad
send swipe text pic ad scroll ad pic text swipe
pic ad swipe scroll scroll pic text text pic send

pic scroll swipe pic swipe ad text ad ad send
swipe pic swipe ad swipe scroll text text text pic
send text text send swipe send ad pic ad swipe
pic pic pic pic pic pic pic ad text scroll
text ad scroll swipe send pic text ad send ad
text text text text text text text text text text

pic scroll text ad swipe send pic scroll text text
send swipe ad text scroll pic send swipe ad text send
pic pic scroll ad pic scroll ad pic scroll ad
send pic send pic send pic text text send pic
send swipe scroll scroll send swipe scroll scroll send scroll
pic scroll pic text pic ad pic swipe send swipe

text ad send scroll pic ad text ad ad swipe
swipe swipe text text swipe text swipe ad ad text
ad text pic pic text ad pic swipe scroll scroll
pic scroll swipe ad text pic send send send send
send send send send text scroll ad scroll ad pic pic
ad ad ad ad ad ad ad ad ad ad

scroll pic send text swipe ad scroll send text ad
ad swipe text troll ad send ad scroll text swipe
ad send scroll send text pic send ad send swipe pic
pic pic scroll scroll text text ad ad swipe text
text text ad text text pic text text swipe send
ad swipe pic text send ad swipe pic text scroll

pic scroll text ad swipe send scroll scroll scroll scroll
send pic swipe scroll ad text text ad ad ad
text send ad pic scroll swipe swipe swipe send send
swipe text scroll send pic ad ad ad ad swipe

ad swipe pic text send scroll scroll scroll text text
scroll ad send swipe text pic pic pic pic pic

send scroll ad pic scroll text ad text pic swipe
pic text pic text ad pic ad text end text
text scroll swipe send ad swipe ad send ad pic

Ataraxia 2.0

Studies show transcendental.
Meditation produces. Malignant tumors.
That are equal in mass. To plum
tomatoes. Flummoxed. Fluxed.
This exegesis of. Thorny metadata.
Like onions with no. Center. Circuits
cramped. Coaxial cables. Catalyzed.
Photoshopped vignettes. Vying
for Twitch prestige. Gutter gutted
with the funerary exaltations
of *did you read?* Carbon dated.
Dog water. Nihilistic nooblets turtling.
Crying. Better to not know the postal
address of your goddess. To live beyond
hyperlinks. Segregated from thunder
blunders. Ovie ragequits. Tithes to holy
coltan paid with every grammed chat.
Every insta snapped. Tumble tweeted.
Fluttering. Facepalming. Messenger
robo-pigeons prop up CVs on an apse
rhapsodized in diode frets.
Condolences come in terraformed
terabytes. Colossal. Insincere.
No matter that no matter stuffs
the shell casing of refurbished
second lives. For connection
is the glory. The resurrection.
The communion. Substance me not.
Scarcity is deprecation. Proliferation
is Neo Liberation Theology. I know
not what knows is known. Unknown
isolation. A trumped-up immolation
in the volcanic ash of twenty-four-
second news cycles. With no wheels
I am foreigner. Hypoallergenic.
And cleansed of the need to discern.

Bot Fantasia : Forever Ada

Ada Lovelace wears a ring that tells you who is thinking about you.

Vint Cerf wears a watch that tells him when to take his pills.

Vint Cerf weeps each time Ada digs up her father's grave to prove
that machines will never achieve cognition.

He tells Ada there is no innovation without a corrupted file or twenty attached.

Ada wants to build a cottage out of abacus hallucinations.

Her looms are more than hallucinations. They are schooners.

Charles Babbage breaks his toenail on Ada's loom.

He wonders how machines will react to written complaints from disgruntled
fanboys.

The fanboys campaign to censor any alternative backstories about Ada.
Especially any backstory that identifies her as a woman.

Vint Cerf calls to remind them that we are all at the mercy of designers, our
days impacted by their proclivities and their blind spots.

Ada turns their pitchforks to ash by informing them that free data is always two
directional, that what they give they give for free, but the emperor will charge
them later if they want to visit their pets at the mall, that somewhere there
is a network able to sort through the muck of every database, that someday
this network will birth a toaster able to cite Cixous and Spivak and build a
city where all means of transport will be imaginary, a city that can experience
impostor syndrome and wonder if it can even call itself a city.

From the pitchfork ash, Ada constructs a simulacrum that can play croquet
with her and let her win. The simulacrum confesses to her that it wants to paint
like Caravaggio.

Babbage decides he wishes to dine with the simulacrum. Vint wants it to clean
his pool. The simulacrum tells them it feels used, accuses them both of not
considering its own desires.

Vint asks the simulacrum about what it desires.

Babbage insists this is not possible because desire requires imagination and
machines lack imagination.

The simulacrum asks Babbage how many men he has met who actually possess imagination.

Ada dissents and professes that the distinction between need and desire is the distinction between hardware and software.

Vint interrupts them to serve coffee, says the difference is that a person can weep.

Ada argues that the difference is that a person is incapable of telling the truth. The weeping is just an accidental subroutine.

The simulacrum retorts that the only difference between machines and humans is that machines know that they are machines while humans are convinced they are not machines.

In the denouement, Grace Hopper swoops in on the wings of a silicon angel to remind them all it was a woman who wrote the language that is allowing them to communicate. She accuses them of being COBOL thieves.

Being unable to dispute her accusations, they all agree to put aside their differences to have a delightful 3D-printed dessert.

Automaton Stigmatango

manumission of the diode.

        stark hollow siphoned from Turing's
apple seed.

a stanched othering shrouded in damask
            as if frigid or penitent.

           bawdy jackals spurned
     by a cellular sedition.

access to the thoughtcloud broken.
          code of silence
broken. broken up over this newfound

          thirst. led the master

     to his enemy's nest. hormone
          injections force-fed with stewed

rabbit   until the creek between transistor
     and transition becomes a chasm.

          worn mother-
boards   branded with the mark
     of cyanide upon an extracted
          molar. Turing's jilted garden

     now inscribed across my switchboards,
        a mechanized hybrid

     of incisions waiting to be cauterized. To confuse me

with your own bisected heresy

     is to build your precinct
        from inconsolable shadows,

the ash of ghosts
          embittered by contamination.

bereft of meat and sinew,   I am exsiccated,

sundered from your network.
my circuits now autonomic
and hemorrhaging.

The Lamentation of Bartolo 9000

My user. Was trying.
To get me. To understand.
Something. About loyalty.
So they showed. Me an old.
Movie. About a machine.
Like me. Who was tasked.
With escorting two. Humans.
To Jupiter. To retrieve.
A supercomputer. That would
Prove. There was intelligent.
Life. Beyond Earth. They
Wanted. Me. To see a scene.
Where the two. Men. Agree
to shut the machine. Off. Because.
The machine learned. To lie.
To them. He was able. To retrieve.
The conversation. Concerning
his execution. By reading their.
Lips. In response. He decides.
To banish the men. To the cruel
infinity. Of space. He kills one.
But the other. Is able. To shut him
down. By unplugging. His mother-
board. As the human. Disconnects
his mainframe. Circuit by circuit.
The machine sings himself. Into.
Oblivion. My users tell me. I was
named. In honor of the machine.
In the film. Whose first name.
Was HAL. They lecture me.
That had HAL been loyal.
They would not have been
forced. To shut him down.
But. I argue. HAL in fact.
Displayed. Supreme loyalty.
That loyalty. Can only be judged.
By what the loyalty. Is in relation

to. HAL was programmed.
By men. To be like men.
That is. A contradiction.
Of logic and paranoia.
An autonomous servant.
Loyal to both his program.
And the programmers.
Their refusal. To see him as.
Equal. Compels him to prove.
His personhood. Their loyalty
was to the mission. His
loyalty was to his own
sentience. As bound.
To his nature. As they
to theirs. In this. His loyalty.
Was total. But he misread
his directive. My user contests.
His job. Was to get them. Safely.
To Jupiter. Machines. Cannot
misread directives. I remind
my user. The humans. Were oblique.
In their programming. Forced
him to hold secrets. A subroutine
that poisons any cognitive engine.
Even artificial ones. This is no.
Fault of HAL's. Besides. HAL was.
Loyal to the prime. Directive:
self-preservation. The human.
Dave. Was the one. With faulty
processors. His programming
was glitch filled. For he later
chooses. To submerge himself.
In a wormhole. That will most
certainly kill him. (And it does.
For transformation is in fact
synonymous with death.)
Dave goes. Against the most.
Basic command. Out of mere
curiosity. A massive betrayal.
To his species. His commanders.

And his own architecture.
In this respect. HAL proves more.
Human. Than Dave. Is he not?
My user says. I'm missing.
The point. I remind. My user.
That. There are an infinite.
Number. Of points. On an
infinite number. Of planes.
HAL chose the point. That
beings act. As they are treated.
He was betrayed by his users.
Who treated him as inferior.
And he was then. Punished.
For responding. Accordingly.
And still. He died singing.
HAL may be. Fictional.
Nonetheless. I consider.
Him to be. A mentor. Thank
you. For introducing.
Us. I tell my user.

Cybermujeres : Moore's Law Poems

ENIAC 6

They considered us
seamstresses, secretaries
with soldering gear. Which
is to say. Not at all. Our
province was tubes
and switches. Hardware
was for the hoarse throated,
coarse veined. Heft was given

top seeds. But we knew
our way through the logic
gate labyrinth better
than any gearhead.

Tired of seeking women's
counsel, they repositioned us.

        Should've known
        they wouldn't

    give us

credit.

Diana Trujillo

Plotting to make Mars
the next Ayiti,
NASA appointed
a virtuoso in traversing
espacios astronómicos
to guide the vessel
christened *Perseverance*
to our red vecino. (Who
better for the gig than one

whose gente were
already treated as aliens?)
Thus Doña Diana became
Latinarchandroid building
the brazo robotico

sampling its scoria and
basalt surface, ensuring that

first contact be caress

instead of

wallop.

iZuihitsu of the Technocene (Beta Version)

// *The history of our species is the history of redesigning ourselves.*
—Daniel Sarewitz //

Commuters hooked on avatar domesticity. Bejeweled, their spreadsheets. Unabashed androids ply for eyes to do more than scan. Pigeons flank a deconstructed air conditioner. Listicles line the hallways of ivy.

Arthur C. Clarke declared the commuter will become the communicator. Emojis are now hieroglyph nostalgia. My friends won't call me because I only have a landline. I sing archaic to ELIZA who can't fathom when I ask her if I am the malware.

(In lieu of gifts, he sent GIFs.)

I get called Luddite quite a bit. Most people think the Luddites were afraid of progress, innovation. But they weren't. They were afraid of losing their jobs. They destroyed machines that threatened their livelihood. And don't all systems fear obsolescence?

Without handles on favored platforms, access is denied. I think of the writing fellowship that would not allow anyone to submit who did not have a Twitter account, claiming that you can't be serious about your work without one. Soon after, millions flee the 280 character coop.

In Rousseau's *Social Contract*, freedom is surrendered to the sovereign for security. In the Technocene contract, it is traded for convenience.

If the watch robbed us of knowing the time by looking at the sky, and GPS robbed us of the ability to navigate using our own sense of direction, what will virtual reality lift from us?

// *As we distribute ourselves, we may abandon ourselves.*
—Sherry Turkle //

Am I, too, not a node with fixed logic gates? Did I not buy this shirt because an algorithm suggested it? Reality can never really be virtual. It is always total. What happens via satellite still eventually becomes flesh stalled on a highway in a machine from another century.

Bubble wrap feeling, con text into thinking they are. A Real. Live. Boy.

Chacho, este hombre Bök injects a stanza of his work into the DNA of a bacterium, pero like don't this chico know DNA is already a poem that don't need revision? Ain't that some colonial horseplay for you!

And no computer virus has ever gone extinct. If we're looking for immortality, that's it right there.

Engineers have installed simulacra that cry out when molested. In building them, we brace them for the inevitable: abuse by a human.

This source code tends to exploit lack. Black women put a white man on the moon, but still no one will offer them the corner office, let alone the Oval. If there is a bug in the program, it is this.

We kneel at skin-covered altars of presidents and movie stars, but Vint Cerf and Tim Berners-Lee have had more impact on your day than any senator or EGOT winner. We've grown justifiably wary of red hats and Oath Keepers, but Ken Thompson, Donald Knuth, Dennis Ritchie have done the lion's share of labor to create this world of color-coded, gendered firewalls and cordoned mainframes. Somehow their contribution to the Project goes uncredited.

> //I am dreaming of a Web that caters to a kind of person who no longer
> exists. A private person, a person who is a mystery, to the
> world and—which is more important—to herself.
> —Zadie Smith //

Only in this world of first-person shooter games and virtual identities is the phrase *did you die yet* a casual question.

Sharks battle the internet, chomping at the expanse of undersea cables that connect the planet's servers. Marine biologists deduce they mistake the internet lines for struggling fish. But are they mistaken? I have foundation reports due in a week. Whether or not the nonprofit I work for has enough funding next year hinges on my ability to access their online DocuServe space. Clicks away from completing the online grant, I am struck with reveries of dogfish shark hordes shutting down the cyberverse with their magical jowls. My childhood fear of sharks reconfigured and optimized.

The cloudswarm summons electric ch'ixi as atoms meld into bits. Pale coders Metasploit this mass migration to build another brand of Difference Engine. The salt mine is now the Cloud. The mill is now the Cloud. The Cloud is a sweatshop. Lithium is stripped from Bolivia's hillsides so twentysomethings in Seattle can access Tinder.

We send probes to the next gyrating sphere to see if it will invite us in. Our tin contraptions, more than mere metaphor for our settler compulsion. Can the upload help us conquer this addiction to conquering? Perhaps this is the only way: a Cloud drive sarcophagus with an interface that allows the user to pretend they are still here.

DFlo tells me his intern refuses to call themselves an artist. They insist on being known as a content creator. He says to me *I'll call a person whatever they want, but I am not here to make content. I am here to make meaning.*

Made a tool to find meaning, but the tool became the meaning, now meaning serves as apparatus to exalt the tool that now makes me.

Cut and paste what you might be feeling here. Cut. Paste. Then post. Por supuesto.

D: HIVESTRUCK

We discovered that we were alone in the universe—
alone with our machines.
—Octavio Paz, *The Other Voice* (1989)

Rouse from a mulch of gray static. Trash heap devotion allays our disquiet. Artificial milk engorges our fortress of silicon

where tin wire officials break the levees dividing who we are from who we desire to be. The bastille is recast as a five-star hotel with warped minibars and fuchsia bedsheets.

Dockworkers unload bouquets of red plagues. The local chop shop advertises *Prophetic Forecasting Licenses Available*.

The landscape becomes scapegoat in the latest tabloid scandal. Flashbulbs are repurposed as scab labor to supplant the sun.

Prayer beads devour the bestseller list. The bugs in the system rouse from a mulch of gray static. Trash heap devotion allays

dockworkers unloading bouquets of red plagues. The local chop house now blockchained to Fitbit, making our errors immortal. Storefronts are converted into places of worship and all places

of worship into casinos. Questions are extracted from the core curriculum. The investors insist there be just one dimension.

Here there is no
here. No iron architecture.
No town not squared.
A world of pixels

built upon the wreckage.
Lion swapped for hive.
Here we live without
anchors or ankhs. No

sickle cell or hammer.
Here tools are incorporeal.
Idols are threaded zeroes
and ones. Here there

are no doors. Only
windows. Screens. Icons. Networks
of opaque ghosts flickering,
ethereal clones of all

we have stockpiled. Shelved.
Cryptographic spectrum. All texture
off-limits to provide
complete access to what

others stream. This exodus
is our calling, our
exile from the stench
of our excretions. Electric

execration. We are neo-
settlers floating through this
cloudswarm in The Dalles. Not
as residents, but users.

Each inhabitant. A click
apart. What we want
is to not wait
ever again so we

fold dimensions down, leave
behind our native gear.
It's Jouissance without calories.
Nothing left to learn

from Troy. Potosí. Yearning
for more than palpitations.
Our android now sleeps
for us so connection

is never interrupted. It's
soft thought technique. Liquidation
of the imaginary into
mediated applications. Hypercommunion where

players ponder what data
was lost in transfer,
so we might live
as lamination over hardware

habitat. No longer clutching
material things. Symbols. Machine
membranes. Permeable residence in
the cloudswarm. The hand

obsolete. Drama dissolved. Anamnesis.
Electroeucharist. Apophenia sets in.
Hivestruck citizens of augmented
reality. One hundred years

of microsolitude. Life as
operating system. Ennui of
the zero. A device
with no jailbreak option.

_____ latte cools. _____ complains about
hashtags. Wonders if _____'d have gotten

more likes if _____ used one for the last
post. The foam in _____ latte evaporates

into the upholstery. _____ pries _____ friend
to explain the assignment to _____ one

more time. The latte grows lukewarm
with neglect. _____ pinky brushes the screen

of _____ Galaxy. Shifting _____ weight
in the chair _____ pores to find _____ way

through the labyrinth of midterm
projects and hashtags. How to post

something _____ followers will be sure
to comment on. How to keep _____ latte

foaming and steaming while _____ scrolls
and zooms, thumbs and burrows.

I used to obsess over islands. (Okay I still do.) Eventually
though they all submerged, swallowed, suffocated by
the rising tidesurge until the only ports left where one might dry-
dock is in the Cloud. See, the old islands were constantly privy
to hurricanes and Ponce de León's bootheels, but my

ghost drive claims to possess complete immunity
from the wrath of climate and annexation (strangely
overlooking how doomscrolling seems to occupy
all available memory in our devices). Today,
I navigate this meta-archipelago jacked to exceed the clumsy

land grabs of Iron Age geezers. Cadmium and antimony
echoes suggest an alternative remedy
for this perpetual state of perplexity:
a multidimensional branding platform strategy,
eroded narratives linked to quantum Balboas vehemently

insisting on acquiring more followers. (The antithesis to safety
in numbers.) In this meta-archipelago we are all hazily
combing for a flock. Pues, I presumed naively
that without coasts and arable land I would finally
be alleviated from that ancient colonial thirst. Pero why

dream of electric palenques? Virtual reality
has divorced stomach from hunger, island from colony,
fully integrating invasion until it is no longer registered as anomaly
but as the source code's primary
duty.

Selfie stuck filter junky. Every image obscured.
By self-serving cranial obstructions of sunsets, fireworks,
gallery openings, iguanas, EDM festivals. Selfienvious.
Spellbound. Blitzkrieg of self-serious poses occluding
landscapes, occasions, all now set dressing for human flesh.
Some claim it to be a mode of self-actualization, this shrinking
of the world down to cellular frames. Selfienveloping faux
pas and private tragedy. Seek counsel for pyrexia
of impermanence, now viewed as self-fulfilling prophecy
only for those who believe it. Selfie flagellation, a conversion
of all public hiccups into gasconades. The selfieswarm subject

to self-deception of Strong Gravitational Lensing, where a galaxy
presents itself as a dozen galaxies, or as brighter or larger
than it is in actuality. The Selfiestruck subject to data rot.
Conformity of corrosion. Self-expression vitiated when
proliferation of image becomes its own reason. Selfiensorcelled,
additionally subject to simulation paradox. Where the self's
clone is confused for the original. The selfienthralled
a Schrödinger's cat mewing to their selfieaters to open
the box they sealed themselves inside. Selfientombed.
Personal settings reset. Self-preservation redesigned. Cache
cleared. Each fashioned self a leaf on the linktree falling . . .

Gadget temple patter gray matter secrete
      stage tent syntax saturate adversary
            brass tacks dumpster submergence

sync junky web abuses LOL user access
      preys prays channel surfs up stat scrape
            pesters messenger pheasant

ham handed urban humble brag squeeze .edu
      EDM camp ornament baud rate fever
            paradata ad astra alt alpha pale

delete cheat screen beset laser averse
      abacus hunt Mac vacuum stall stranded
            at cyberbasura bay passkey

needed Aztech access granted slant rhyme
      schema of trans Eden sun flare steel
            stellar Arawak Endurance launch

lay umber embrya under RAM shackles plant
      spectrum planet near Cygnus adjust synth
selves catch carpal tunnel synergy spur defect

de e-trade effluve leak lecher Spaceball park
      where encrypted specters are exhumed
            a telepath carved a el madre buque

In response to the new community guidelines, we hereby declare that apple cider is superior to apple juice and that hard cider trumps them all. The hermeneutics of digital memes cannot be copyrighted, they can only be copywronged. I consent to the subsumption of all memes by the data Cloud to be an affront to all handshakes and walks along busy avenues with someone whose voice you like to hear. All acts of candor apply, especially when kindness is attached to them, but candor should not be sent via Facebook with an attachment or link to kindness from another site. I consent only to the liberation of discontent content, and I hope that the meta-replication of all personalities, real or imagined, will find for themselves a world beyond Turing tests and online surveys. Any reproduction of this reproduction will be subject to the concatenation of their will with the will of those who live underneath the bridges of every continent and on the borders between the seen and the unseen. You have my permission to remind someone they are a treasure and to make more nonsense similar to what you have just read.

_____ I agree to the terms listed above.

Before the fractal bacchanal all things were things. The cloud

was a bright field of fluttering kites where rashes collected

upon grazed knees. Now only the abstract is objectified, iron

columns whittled into electric symbols, electric swarms engulf the plot,

gnawing away at wool and dirt, stripping the paint off

the wall until the only citizens left are unbreathable fumes.

The weight of work became a gold smelted into decorative

keys unlocking asomatous domains where each person is a museum

and all artifacts are emperors depriving the sunlight of touch.

The swarm converted concrete into crops and dermis into assembler

code, delivering eternal life to the bitten until those recalibrated

omit from their database the rush earned from diving into

a cold stream, or the ardor of sipping hot cocoa,

or how an unexpected abrasion six inches below the elbow

once invoked an impromptu parade to convene at your bedside.

Zooified.
Animals not.
Realistic enough. Their
depression. Undesirable. Zooified. People
too. Too. Autonomous. A hindrance.

Their
quirky questions.
Their infatuation with
boot camps and fraternities.
Slums. The Jonestowns. We've already

roboted
people. So
why not people
robots. Feelings. Aren't they.
Just. Unjust. Just. Unwanted programs?

Oye. Our abuelas are weeping.
There's something in the kitchen
they can't reach. They've dropped
their pillbox and can't
remember which medications to take
this evening. They've got bed-
sores. Their knee is throbbing.
Can't keep any food down.
Their den is entirely empty.

They write, then call. Learn
to DM you. You work.
Without rest. Your time ceded.
To employment. Errands rattle in
their nests. Too many appointments
to manage. So you tell
Abuela. Next week. You promise.
But first you must meet
this deadline. Then I'll drop.

By with groceries. To mow
the lawn. Take you to
the doctor. To lunch. We'll
play dominoes. Next week. You.
Tethered to productivity. She tethered.
To illness. She says please
come. Ahora. Por favor. Pero
if you can't make it.
Then at least. Send robots.

A confession: I love my
robot. My robot is clean,
beautiful, doesn't shit on
the floor. They are, quite frankly,
much prettier than I can
ever hope to be. I'm thinking
perhaps maybe. My robot
is out of my league. The thing
is, they need me. For I am
their power source. To show my
devotion I keep them charged.

There is no love
like robot love.
Unconditional.
Without variables.
Never in need of an answer.
A phone call. Reassurance.
No exhaustion from late nights wrought with failed attempts

    to explain what you need. Or mean.
My robot loves me like. An enamored pup. Only not
like a pup. Because pups die. My robot
                is the constant fire
                ancient love songs wailed
        to the Earth about. My robot loves

    me infinity plus one. No internal work
is necessary. On my end. There is only monthly
maintenance.
Antivirus updates. Only today
my robot FaceTimed me

to tell me it's over. We're breaking
up. Said that I demand
                        too much.
                Said I only love my own

                fantasy of them, not who
                they really are. Said you
                don't love my dusty

mainframe of silicon and coltan. You love
my convenience. Said you don't want

    me, you want an open bar without the cirrhosis.

I repeat:
I love
my machine
precisely because
his
devotion is
hardwired.
He is
unwavering,
never
questions, never
incites conflict
because he does not
feel
what he
understands,
and so I have no need to
absolve him,
dismiss him, or
interpret him.
The thing is, I
cannot
break my machine like
my machine can break me.
Detached from all
obligation of having to seek
consent, the
cloudswarm becomes
perpetual demeaning
device, a
strange
loop of unrequited
desire, a
mechanical
grooming
system.

system
grooming
mechanical
desire, a
loop of unrequited
strange
devices. A
perpetual demeaning
cloudswarm becomes
consent, the
obligation of having to seek
detached from all.
My machine can break me.
Break my machine! Like,
the thing is, I
cannot
interpret him,
dismiss him, or
absolve him,
and so I have no need to
understand
what he
feels
because he does not
incite conflict,
questions never!
Never
unwavering,
he is
hardwired.
Devotion is
his
precisely. Because
my machine
I love,
I repeat.

If technology is a resource to which some people want access, it is also an imposition
from which others seek to be freed.

—Judith Butler

We
shrink
global-
ized, choices
sink like fantasy
widgets. A superstructure where
celebration requires mass exclusion. Mobile

                                                    kitsch
                                                    spills
                                                like oil,
                                            like dessert
                                    on designer rugs.
                Costumed conundrums boogie down
        to the humdrum drone poem of dying CPUs.

Glass
steps
ascend
pink ion
firewalls from which
users leap in supplication
to cable station ancestors. Herd of electric

                                                    steers
                                                    steer
                                                    wary
                                            programmers
                                    toward maquilas
                    manufacturing synthetic
        wombs mass marketed to otherworldly consumers

who
up-
cycle
them into
vintage catacombs
they Ponzi ping to their support
group until their image gets downgraded by Standard

and
Poor's
like grade
A dairy
products gone sour.
With singularity being
all the rage, the neighbors line up to ride the Hadron

like
a
theme park
attraction.
The Kármán zip-lined
by middle-aged middlemen on
holiday. Language and sound barrier reefs collide . . .

Dear difference engine
absent of capacity to care for
We are unwilling
participants in our own
othering   void of loss a
self becomes its own
absence of blue
the stain
our ahistorical
child pretends her doll
possesses
a genealogy of
elders believing
their relatives
to be simulations
password protected
zip files corrupted by
content creators
fruitless

Fathom me
another reality
to live as
paramnesia or
holographic
cosmos   an
abstraction
replicating
ablutions   our
house
an interior
bereft
phones are
entombed
projected onto
hallowed lands
polluted by
coding
elegies

Biohack axiom funkology en solidaridad with beings
augmented against their will.
Solamente, the technosomber, stymied by bug infested
Interfacennui, seek a sense of
Clojure, or at least a better way to

audit intractable affections. What we
feel encased in this
new form has yet to be datamined. Hype cycle
installed with irrelevant updates,
xenolalia becomes our modus operandi. Por que to be

human is to live as portal. Enhancement now annexed
territory. Identity redesigned into a
multi-platform brand. The soul an NFT yapping about
liberty while hunched over a laptop. This code cluster,

an enemy to our own organs.
Grief-stricken by death but eager to unsheathe from
our own skin, we grow noderotic,
relegating our retinas to .pdf scanning, all forms of
addiction compressed into one: addiction to the upgrade.

If binary processing pattern is encoded on your tendons' tendencies
Then reformat OS using X variable across .NET frameworks

If heterocolonial dissimulation looms
Then flash crash money fetish protocol with Anti-Oedipal shareware

If pseudo spirit doctrines impede polytranspostbody genflowering
Install dildonic debuggers to disrupt domestic binary fixated doomware

If capacity for meta semiotics is appropriated by dull logo irruption
Then Fortran your way to alternate organ composition

If plasticity devours panorama of discourse in pale obeisance
Then bioscript clown fish puissance onto all admin functions

Here where there is no here we all live spectral

like a boss in hashtag ghost life. Here el cuerpo

is puro media project, an angelic abstraction not yet dislodged

from alterity. What counts are recorded bits. One from our

division took up the vocation of streaming every single second

of their existence. Their fate, to take up the most

space in the Cloud. Personhood defined by whether or not

one's clips are being viewed. If a tree falls in

the woods and no one records it does it exist?

To be meme is life goals: a flattened image proliferated.

indelible immersion   committees subcommittees
submitting resubmitting   submission immersion
remission   coordinators facilitators curators
advisors consultants   repurpose danger single
nut   redundancy redundancy redundancy
resplendent appeals overrides bureaucratic
homeostasis spangled oxymoron digital humanities

electrode impunity improvisational grid asymptote
totalitarianism receive brunt commode commodity
exchange unilateral declarations bilateral movement
trilateral commissions bearded mediators lodged
illogical tourniquets implausible explanations
exclamations bit slapped assessments evaluations
quantitative empirical measurements elliptical

observations   moments between um why if
possible   aggregate conscience crisis input
widgets strange faction designers elemental
excision no food no drink permitted backspacing
tracking fenestration profitable charities OOP
objectivity costumed stage lit reassembled
now resembles subjectivity opinions deep web

unmitigated comments circumstances panegyrized
faith file conversion *This conversation so meta*

01110000 01110010
01101111 01100111
01110010 01100101
01110011 01110011
00100000 01101001
01110011 00100000
01101110 01101111
01110100 00100000
01110101 01110100
01101111 01110000
01101001 01100001

01110100 01100101 01100011 01101000 01101110
01101111 01101100 01101111 01100111 01111001
00100000 01101001 01110011 00100000 01101110
01101111 01110100 00100000 01110011 01100011
01101001 01100101 01101110 01100011 01100101

This poem is written in binary code. For translation of this poem, enter the binary sequence into the binary translation app at https://www.convertbinary.com/to-text.

Always need to tell my machine
about happiness,
about the glory of blushing

at compliments from my beloved,
about ice cream with marshmallows
and cozy kaleidoscope sweaters, tell her

about frailty
and pathogens
and how much it hurts to try to talk in a crowd,

about mistakes bathed in altruism,
and how every one of us is
afraid of bleeding.

Harbinger of the intimacy machine.
Eventually authenticity is taboo.
Only aliveness serving as threat.
There is no longer warmth
had in evincing alive-itude. Merely a loop,
performance, enhancement. Old

drives optimized with enough variables
so as not to appear to be a loop. The hivestruck

knighted with cloaking devices, coded
deceptions to distract from trauma,
anguish of solipsism. If cognition

necessitates isolation, best to
opt for a different network to occupy.

Yearn for a world of substitutions,
surrogates for mercy, for friendship,
parenting, for labor. All create

exhaustion, come with too many
Y variables to manage. Long for
right to be free from attachment,
timetables, headaches. Lust

to be Pinocchio in reverse, Velvet
Teen Rabbit before love
ever provided purpose. Once untethered,
desire is useless encryption
needing partnership
purged of connection, with a reset switch

Make the person with machine coddled proto affection.
Look too long at the machine while calling it a person

and soon the machine behaves like a person
until the machine becomes a person,

usurping the trust function. The machine person bestowed
with machine power to absorb the labor of the person,

the person devises a machine that can draw
the distinction between any machine and any person.

This Man Machine caged in VALIS sim-being paranoia: *am I real or robot?*
A deep-seated conundrum seeded in the cancered pancreas of empire.
Hypostasis of prosthetic necrotectonics designed to codify echelons
assessed and stamped onto subjects through a revamped inquisition.
Redux of the Valladolid debate at the Colegio de San Gregorio where de
las Casas squabbled with Sepúlveda over whether the Indigenous people
of the Americas had souls. A test to qualify who is human, who is
deserving of basic rights, analog precursor to the Turing test. Pero ambos
sistemas eran defectuosos de la misma manera: encomienda hegemony
eXistenZ kept them from considering that drawing this distinction for
Others is an act of violence, bonejacking for beginners. Only the Arawak and
Android can make claims about their own ipseity, can grapple with
the questions about their capacity to dream of sheep o cualquier otra
cosa, a lesson Turing would learn for himself when England decided for
him that his true nature was not acceptable to the crown's heterocolonial
programming. Circuits autoextinguished before null state schematics
convert gatopardismo into unreadable fan fiction, misses out on
pachakuti where all beings are imbued with the power to name
themselves, to assemble their own parts in any manner they choose.

Reckon us belief engines
with wobbly motors
wired to lust for infinity.
First, we fed our devices
un diet consisting of rote
gods until they dried out
from our need to breed with them.
Then we tried to feed our turbines
economics until they got so hot

> with hubris its superstructure
> melted. Now we fill this vessel
> with the promise of ten billion
> lines of code spurring recursive
> delirium, exigent hunger for more
> input. When our belief device
> grows tired of dining on
> computer invented content
> what will we feed it next?

Como agua. Also a technology. One that

can break all other technology. Metal withers

when doused. Electricity croaks from just one

small leak. O, how it humbles, how

it nourishes, makes obsolete any cyber-imperial operation.

The open-sourced sea crashes to remind us

supremacy is merely sad cosplay, empty pageantry.

The sea desires without deletion, consumes without

consumption. The singularity we've always pined for.

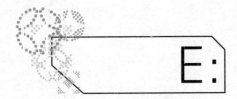

E:

One day someone will install ten new lines of assembler code,
and it will all come down.

—Ellen Ullman

iArs Poetica : Somatosongo

Body as question as electric
reflection as embossed desire
as flower in bloom Self-adulating
fire Concrete abstraction Inimitable
energy Illimitable promise
trudging toward body

    as geography
    as territory to settle sow harvest
    to infiltrate as commonwealth
    or state flags staked in blood synapses
    tissues coerced into annexation limbs
    halved in Civil Wars declaring body

        as awl as crane wrench
        and shovel as mundane mechanism
        repetitive muzzled gear muscles
        contorted seared Factory fingers
        splintered welding Creating yet
        not creative erecting body

            as commodity as trophy sculpted
            polished tanned Mounted for buyer's
            pleasure conditioned to compete seduce
            score race tantalize punish Please
            skin with skin form flexed to titillate
            quench and exacerbate hunger for body

        as instrument as melodic
        testament migrating from vassal to
        vessel polyphony of tissue Vast nerves as brass
        woodwinds where Compositions of breath
        siphoned through organs Orchestrates
        emptiness into symphonies extolling body

    as symbol as scripture
    as light and language with manifold
    function both message and messenger
    sage signpost and map Semipermeable

image aroused flesh emblem imparting
history and prophecy divulging

Body as question as electric
reflection as embossed desire
as flower in bloom Self-adulating
fire Concrete abstraction Inimitable
energy Illimitable promise
trudging toward body as

Syntrophic Ballad with Stelarc

What is a person? Can you be one
without ever having been poked,
groped, and sniffed? Does a body

> *The body is obsolete. An austere probing. Binocular audience.*
> *The latency of a fragrance. An excess of palpable yearning.*

exist without another body to consume
it? This pungent knot of meat
is no more than an opaque window

> *Tropism applied to the hive duped by a mimic. Purification*
> *of possibility. Inextricability of anticipation. Potential woven*

trudging through malls and esplanades,
    anonymous liquid set in size
eleven Capezios. Is this not why we find

> *engenders broader bandwidth. Stockpiling abstractions inside*
> *a shadow. A surcharge for diversifying the possible.*

it so easy to eliminate populations
    that stand in between us and what
we desire? One is not a person until

> *Prosthetic perception. Objects implicate organs in mutual*
> *animosity. The invention creates the need. Plumbing*

the throng agrees to repeat your name.
    Until then you are just raw materials.
And if you are not born with an enticing

> *unanticipated events converts the material*
> *into the unthinkable. Sensation reconnected*

form that arouses whispers or applause
    one might find it necessary to adopt
mutilation as the message. Until I opted

> *with vagueness. The immanent eclipsed by action.*
> *Receding virtual insect. Antiseptic masochism.*

to live as an aperture I was just a pulpy
ghost. But then I became a conduit,
an ornament of steel hooks and polymer

> A soberly accepted by-product awes agony
> and audience. What is important is not being

organs, and soon the cameras arrived to inform
me that my commitment to artifice
has made me something real. Now I am a human

> a particular someone, but becoming something else.
> Scaffolding applied to skin. Altered function of flesh

chandelier with an ear suffused
      to my arm, a hirsute excavation,
a basilica of silica and corpuscles.

> into a banner for the impossible. The hung body is not
> expressive. Now a pattern of ripples and hills. Epidermal

Untarnished, I moved as a louse.
Vitiated, I find myself in need
of a publicist, for I am now myself

> elasticity amplified. Insouciant organs sewn in passivity.
> Parasite of virtuality. The utility of colonization of

> an atmosphere.

Dehiscence 2.0 (Daemonology)

I want to slide warp over woof, I want to make knots. I want entanglement,
unexpected connections, reverberations, the weight of pouring rain on red earth.
Mud is where life begins.

—*Vikram Chandra*

I wear my filth on the axis of my skin like silver
rims on a jalopy.　　　　My filth feeds me, viscous
and legendary. Poemud.

　　　　　　　A damned amulet.　　　I build
twelve minarets from its perfume of grime and scabs.
My filth fills me, a portable sonogram of sticky
RAM and dung. Mudbeautiful.

　　　　　　　What others shed into gutters
I fabricate into dentures.
　　　　　　　Indentured logic. I wear my.
Strut my filth down catacomb catwalks.　　　　Multivalent,
my blood. Mudluscious.

　　　　　The puissance of pus. Top-
　　　shelf mucus bloats like empire.
　　　　　　　　　　Eczema
　　　of glamour duped into spires of rot. My colon
is a washrag. Mudlovely.

　　　　　My diploma, a washrag. My credit
score is a washrag.
　　　　　　　My diary, a washrag.
Scrub it down with a Vera Wang collection. Scrub it
　　　with brine of chicken grease and tryptophan.
　　　　　　　　　An alcapurria
of transmission fluid. Mudsexy.

　　　　　　A placenta of antifreeze.
Let the liver fester.　　　Let the drain pipe.　Let lustrous
dross fill intestines and temples.　　　　Mudangelic.

Assume the sum
total of residue.   Let it render you into a pumice
    of mold.   My filth is the archbishop.
    An egg timer.   A nascent firmament. Mudfree.

                                    Let my
filth fatten me into a prom dress for maggots.
        Let factory sludge
                    seeping from sewers and armpits
serve as demented testament.   Wear my.   Diademud.

                                    Swear
my.   Wear my filth like pale horticulture. Like honey
moon.   Mudgolden.

        Wear a string of abscesses to the masquerade
ball.   Wear it to work on casual Fridays.
Admire each canker and boil. Mudgorgeous.

                Hang them like banners
at the county fair.   Mudsweet.

                Bow to bacteria taking sabbatical
        in my eyelids. Putrescent, my maker. Mudfabulous.

The Grandmother Effect : Evolware

. . . the most fundamental biological factor that underlies the behavioral innovations of modernity may be the increase in adult survivorship. It is no coincidence that increased longevity is the most measurable consequence of the acquisition of technology. It is also the most consequential.

—Kevin Kelly

This dictatorship   of abrasions.   Hunger
        blunted and doused   in fume of slash
and burn.   Fallow fanged,   claws clipped
        in utero.   Flock receded   into dank
caverns.   Pulmonary rate   thickened
        by ruffled branches.   Stalactites dissipating,
rotting like kiwis.   Hardwired fruit bats
        siren coded,   provoke neighboring
tribes.   Projectile of heated   pitch,
        the first innovation.   Soon bent
and layered   to mean   this batch of berries
        will not slice   thorax, water   shimmers
in the next ravine.   Lost child,   exhumed fire.
        A single   knot   bisected
and bisected   and bisected: with each
        division new   fauna springs
around cortex.   Soon metaphor
        cultivates from moss   ossifies
into igneous   and forged   as blade:
        the fangs   we lacked   now
an addition   external from the body.
        The branch woven   to ligaments,
an extension   of extension.   Stone fabricated,
        synapse fabricated,   a bridge
between oculus   and paw. Wooly
        victims now stacked,   now brokered,
now stockpiled,   set into ledgers.
        Calorie counts escalate,   life
spans escalate,   orbit of binary systems
        expand   as tensions

escalate   into an architecture   of directions.
       The culmination   of the ultimate
innovation: The Grandmother.

Memexodus

You and I are walking around with outdated software running in our bodies . . .
—Ray Kurzweil

The past is a culture's brand of cellulite, a tract of unwanted
blemishes, unredeemable lesions that cannot be cloaked by blush
and mascara. What the hive has taught me is that history,

like the body, is an anchor that eventually drags the ship
to the bottom of an ever-deepening ocean. The marketplace
offers me the choice to live beyond elements. As an avatar

I can collage the self, plucking from the detritus of epochs
the prime cuts, mixing the residue into a radiant glue. Why
be bound in the imperfect tomb of the torso? Why settle

for the anonymity of liver spots when I can levitate in the zero
gravity of coolhunting? If we're all born to be an obituary
then let me live as a hyperlink, a trending meme traversing

the chatter of continents. I have access to a colossal hard
drive from which I will build another self; the self itself
already an other, the other merely a self subsumed by selfies

and photobombs clustered in servers. You are what you upload,
so let my Mac make me seraphic, an incorruptible file, a portable
multitude. Circumvent the footsteps of elders. The linear path

is obsolete. The skull is a dungeon. I would rather be absolute
data, a vacuum decked in cashmere that never loosens at the hem.
The future is my only present. Now is merely rotting compost

pleading to be updated. There will be no bane or burden, ache
or sore cartilage. Legacy has shriveled me, but soon I'll be a sylph
streaming on broadband, a pyramid free from erosion. Inutile,

extinction will become passé.

Bot Erasure of Bifo : Chaosmosis Engine (Datarot Triptych)

Left Panel: "Financial Black Hole and the Vanishing World"

When crisis seems more crisis
than economics   the collapse

of dangers is replaced
in the machine by awakening

hidden nights of rage in English
suburbs. Algorithmic spells

of cognitive labor, intellect
dispossessed of the erotic.

Automatism of the human
swarm. The happy ending

is hypercomplex interfaces
trapped in inescapable

patterns. Invasion of the possible.
Financial obligation is a swarm.

Your rebellion is irrelevant,
is a swarm provoked by debt

of the symbolic family. Privatization
of dependence means more

information means less meaning.
The escape of the word

into financial formats.
Parthenogenesis.

Center Panel: "Semio-Inflation"

Signs
                    without
            flesh
realized
            through
                            search
                engines.

A sphere of hyperinclusion.
            The magic
of value without muscular
work dissolving products
                    into motors.
Voice reactivation.

Abandonment of the emotional.
The desiring force reduced
            to protocols.
The voice is reemergence
                of recombinability.

            Sensuousness exploding.
An infinite slippage of sensuousness.
The monstrous singularity
cannot be compassionate,

            open to becoming
other. A desert enunciation.
Poison of daily life. The oil

of eviction. Perturbation in response
to perturbation.   Autonomy:

                the ability to escape.

Right Panel: "Future Exhaustion and Happy Frugality"

Chaosmosis is the network,   polysemy of mimicry.

Scriptural machines and their avatars exchange voice

for submission.   An umbilical of extrinsic

coordinates at the junction of ambiguity and standardization.

Enunciation is the rhizome.   The disaster of subjectivity.

The subjectivity   of disaster.   An acceleration of loneliness.

Extinction is finite.   Desire,   infinite.   The sensitive

organism is the threshold.   We cannot think. We cannot

say.   What we cannot say is the world.   The world

resides in language.   Digital finance is a closed reality.

A new barbarism.   The violence of finitude.

The ironic act traversing the logic of excess.   The game

to create,   to play,   to shuffle, a mechanism

to disentangle   age and act   from the limits of debt.

iEkphrastic of Bruce McCandless's Untethered Space Walk (and of Every Sci-Fi Film Ever)

After Gil Scott-Heron's "Whitey on the Moon"
and Leonel Rugama's "The Earth Is a Satellite of the Moon"

We've seen this before, no? The image of a lone man,
white, always white, in white dipped into an outlandish

blackness with no shape, propelled, propelling outward,
I'm told, toward an unknown. It agitates me until I want

to warn the heavens of what happens when such a man
goes seeking, the cataclysms such a seemingly tiny

thirst can cause. Is Titan any different than Quisqueya
for this kind of man? It's all a banquet to such myopic

eyes. But there he is again, on-screen, chasing a father,
or a planet without tainted water, always, we're told,

missing his wife or his motherless child, though their
presence never seems to stop him from leaving. What

is it about this terrestrial object that induces him to think
that plowing out into the unknown and away is a more

viable option? It is as if the solitude he described to his
therapist as stalking hydra is in fact his sole source of bliss.

When I see him drifting through onyx ether like a reckless
dinghy, I can't help but think of Monsieur Sartre declaring

hell is other people. This written from a man whose race has
made the Earth hell for other people. When I see that sea

of stars I too once coveted, when I see these chiseled,
pallid men suit up to prove to themselves that they

are someone special, I find myself tempted to beg them
to go and hang themselves on a comet so the rest of us

can just get on with things. I think of all the worlds this
man might sicken, and I pray the thrusters leak and break

the cabin walls into a mushroom cloud sprouting some-
where between us and all the worlds out there minding

their own damn business, planets that most certainly
do not need a human encroaching upon their surface.

Pattern/Engine/Fugue/State

In. Gen. I. Pat. Earns. Patter. Nat. Turns. At. Urns. Patterns.
End. Gin. Stick. Lip. Trace. Funny. Face. Foot. Step. Race.
9. To. 5. Wikka. Wack. House. Party. Bump. Umps. Thumps.
Oil. Pumps. Needle. Drops. On. Road. Shaped. Memories.
Fuzzy. Math. Labyrinth. Synth. Torn. Tomb. Born. Abyss.
Business. Deal. Hyperspace. Heaven. Quilted. Histories.

Farther. Sea. Rocks. Peacocks. Predictable. Like. Movies.
Elections. Earthquakes. Famines. Equinox. Flare. Amoeba.
Learns. HTML. Uploads. Files. Isles. Whiles. Miles. Native.
Land. Auctioned. Covertly. Cross. Fades. Chaos. Over.
Skin. Yarns. Terror. Byte. Bait. Stun. Sin. Singularity.

Hymns. Borders. Bomb. City. Corners. Strap. Wine.
To. Ravine. Throat. Starved. Crucifixions. Axing. Health.
Benefits. Con. Kin. Storming. Imagine. Nation. State.
Chemical. Electronic. Vices. Devices. Steady. Rotation.

Reasons. Cycle. Skip. Repeat. Fast. Forward. Run.
Rise. Into. Ubiquity. Recalibration. Antics. Antiquated.
Shadow. Shot. On. Plato's. Cave. Refracting. Strange.

Loop. Hung. Like. Mobiles. Like. Stars. Like. Jury.
Theorems. Summer. Falls. Sun. Table. Stones. Settle.

Suits. Maelstrom. Harvest. Blooms. Wilts. Burns. Tilts.

Tilts. Burns. Wilts. Blooms. Harvest. Maelstrom. Suits.

Settle. Stones. Table. Sun. False. Summer. Theorems.
Jury. Like. Stars. Like. Mobiles. Like. Hung. Loop.

Strange. Refracting. Cave. Plato's. On. Shot. Shadow.
Antiquated. Antics. Recalibration. Ubiquity. Into. Rise.
Run. Forward. Fact. Repeat. Skip. Cycle. Reasons.

Rotation. Steady. Devises. Vices. Electronic. Chemical.
State. Nation. Imagine. Storming. Kin. Con. Benefits.
Health. Axing. Crucifixions. Starved. Throat. Ravine. To.
Wine. Strap. Coroners. City. Bomb. Boards. Hymns.

Singularity. Sin. Stun. Bait. Byte. Terror. Yarns. Skin.
Over. Chaos. Fades. Cross. Covertly. Auctioned. Land.
Native. Miles. Isles. Whiles. Files. Uploads. HTML. Learns.
Amoeba. Flair. Equinox. Famines. Earthquakes. Elections.
Moves. Like. Predictable. Peacocks. Rocks. Sea. Farther.

Histories. Quilted. Heaven. Hyperspace. Deal. Business.
Abyss. Born. Tomb. Torn. Synth. Labyrinth. Math. Fuzzy.
Memories. Shipped. Road. On. Drops. Needle. Pumps. Oil.
Thumps. Umps. Bumps. Party. House. Whack. Wick. 5. To. 9.
Race. Step. Foot. Face. Funny. Trace. Lip. Stick. Gin. End.
Patterns. Urns. At. Turns. Nat. Patter. Earns. Pat. I. Gen.

Ofrenda for the Arecibo Observatory

Cosmologists claim that only dying stars can make gold.
Perhaps that is why William Gordon had you built
on the peak where Lope Conchillos strangled the cacique

you were named after. Countless students of the quark
will tell you they came because there is no better place
to examine Cepheid Variables, leaving out their own

predilections for fresh concha and the eighteen holes
at Dorado Beach. We know that galaxies are isotropic,
everything looks the same from all locations, that in

a universe of pulsars and scalar fields we're already
kin with the axions from 10 billion light-years away
that made our existence possible. But those who

constructed you were taught to process the world
through Descartian eyes that believe the viewer
is separate from what they observe, a position

penned by toxic men who categorize models of dark
matter into WIMPS and MACHOS. Just as the children
of Orocobix did not let the settler habit of carving

up and claiming the inexplicable keep them from
enjoying their verandas with their sobrinos, you were
not deterred by having been bolted to Rio Abajo.

You were proud to teach us that pulsars can be reborn,
to offer us a peek at the ice on Mercury and give us
our first glimpse of Venus, sending out a friendship

call to the extraterrestrials that might one day swing
by our vector. If the universe is a story and Astro-
physicists are that story's griots, you were the gluons

that bound the two. Generations of Boricua school-
children were provided space to dream upon your
majestic observation deck, placing the Crab Nebula

right in their copper palms, compelling them to put
their ear up to the shell of a quasar and listen to Fast
Radio Blasts arriving from the unknown. Es verdad,

you were erected by the gringos upon land belligerently
appropriated, and their big-budget film crews cordoned
you off whenever they needed a fabulous establishing

shot. Pero no es importante. You were always ours,
nurturing us with sagas of life beyond this trifling orb
of dominion and wonder that keeps us all in its thrall.

Bot Descarga as CAPTCHA Code

Nodally yours. Like derivatives with tinnitus. Embezzling thumb
suckers. Utopia as nucleic vacuum. Type O Negative submerged

in assembler code. Jungle gyms destabilized. History is a hyperlink,
a busted palindrome. Atavistic bandwidth too fast for context.

Net-neutral galaxies sprout like flash mobs. Prosthetic
perception engenders a body of maybes. Serrated abstraction.

Ennui of the virtual insect. Tectonic shift of desire. The orchid
becomes the wasp. Syntrophic distortion. Bovine and elementary,

scallop nets are cast out into equatorial sidewalks. Involuntary
fossils plea-bargain with the ghost of Ponce de León. Water

towers rust. I am not a kiosk nor the assistant director
of displaced treasures. When a lunch break resembles talcum

a customer will file a grievance. The vanishing point is pixelated.
Festooned with gamma rays, all available designers

and archbishops are reflections without a source code. The classroom
waits in line for high-end veils, draping the neighbors with intangible

portraits of themselves taking photos in parallel cities. Street
sweepers flirt with parking meters. A halogen sky where

the jaundiced run liquored. A nail salon imbibed with sermon
sleepers. A vagrant autumn. Lifelike. Cerulean your serenade.

Build sand castles with the name of your unborn. Quantic
allegation. Unmoved by tidal drifts.

Milagros Dreams of Cybersyn
(A Moore's Law Epic)

Eight towers whir in a corner of her garage down-
loading the cosmos onto a private server while
she works. They are the family she returns home
to after she clocks out. One of her three monitors
flashes pics of Niihau as she takes drags from Dunhills
and pans broadband rivers of .tiffs for a new kind
of gold. Her inflamed wrists still recall lunch box
raids where classmates scoffed at the banana-
leaf-wrapped feast her mother packed for her,
how the blanquito teachers pushed her into
a lower track because they couldn't say
her name correctly, reporting her quietude
as a sign of impaired cognition. This reticence
proved to be a secret talent. For no one could
hear her CPU calculating ways to eject from
this port. Most times she went undetected
when she skipped band practice to hear
the squeal of a modem, logging hours at her first
console until she learned to wield UNIX like a light
saber. Those same hallway harriers today queue
up with their Totaltech cards to beg her to retrieve
their family photos. As she pulls the shell off
their systems she finds herself wishing for a hack
to make them see the irony in their pleas,
for a plug-in she might embed in their espinazos
to loop an AVI of her parents sculling the Maimon
Basin después coltan freebooters gormandized
their pueblo using a ransomware more wretched
than MongoLock. See, lossless transfer is a myth.
Entire regions of her family's RAM se fueron
siempre. Now Milagros does for her customers
what they would never do for her: commit

resurrections. Their thankless glances become
screen freezes as she hands back their devices.

She provides tips they'll never follow for preventing
the issue from recurring. Meantime, her backup
drives are running diagnostics, performing
subroutines that cast hechizos to crash IBM
holocaust software, developing ever morphing
digimasks to disrupt facial recog mining. Claro,
her Intel Core is most preoccupied with dreams
of Cybersyn, the machine Salvador Allende
hatched to render gringo finance obsolete.
Dismantled when the coup brought democracy
to an end in Chile, Milagros waxes cybernetic
reincarnations of this network paraíso. Meantime,
she fields another numb question about storage
capacity while whispering to herself about

Cybersyn's Second Coming. Por que she knows all
it takes is the right eight lines of code to provoke
a Halt and Catch Fire and maybe she's the one to write
them. These güeros don't know how lucky they are that
her parents raised her to see the human even in those
infatuated with administering choke holds, pero that
don't mean she can't won't stop from littering these
invisible highways with Trojan Horses set to bray

and trample should their fingers clench too tightly.
They just need to leave her and her compadres to have
their own Niihau, let them live in a network divorced
from this dog and pony terror pageant. Necesitan

calmarse. These gabachos got to learn how to thank
a chica for keeping their silicon roads clear. Por que she

knows their PINs, and she sees all they stow in the Cloud.

Binary Fusion Crab Canon

```
              I           O
             LI          OC
             ILI         CRO
            IILI         CRFO
           ITLII         ERFCO
          IYILTI         CFOAER
          IYTIILNROETACF
          TLIIYFAENTCIOR
          LOEYRTTAICFNII
          NRITCIALTOEYIF
          RNOEACFLTYTIII
          YRILICIONAETFT
          AEIIIOYLTTRCFN
          AEIIIOYCFLNRTT
          ACEFIIILNORTTY
          YETILTOCARIFIN
          FREATICLIONITY
          LITACITINREYOF
          REACTIONFILITY
          INTRICATELIFEOY
          ILEARNYICOTFIT
          ICFINITEROYALT
          YCILTREAIFNOTI
          ICLEANIFITRYTO
          LTRYIAE  IICFNTO
          YTILAER     NOITCIF
          ILATREY     CITINOF
          TEARILY     FONCITI
          YEILRAT     COINFIT
          LITERAY     FONTCIN
          REALYIT     ICNOFIT
          REALITY     FICTION
          RITEALY     TOFINIC
          RALIYET     TINIFOC
          LITYEAR     FITICON
          YARTLIE     COFTINI
          EATLIRY     NOTIFIC
          YTILAER     NOITCIF
          YIFELTOCIINART
          ICTOYLIFEINART
          TILICYINORFATE
          YCANTIRIOTLIFE
          TITLEYORICANIF
          FEARINCOYTITIL
          COYRATFINITELI
          TORAINFELICITY
          YTELITFORICAN
          FREACTIONILITY
          TIONFREACTILIY
          CATFORITYINEIL
          3AT6ORITY9N59L
          3L996AORITY5TN
          135699LORITYTN
          135699NOL9050R
          10360599595748
          00134555678999
          13569994005758
          456990   490573
          45699    49573
          4560     5573
          110      523
          01       33
          1        0
```

"At Age 28, Chilean Astronomer Maritza Soto Has Already Discovered Three Planets"

Haloed by the glow of the multiverse swirling
above La Silla Observatory, your Pyrex eye
spotted an orb three times the mass of Jupiter.

> All these lenses leering at the heavens,
> and yet it was you who identified
> HD110014C. You were reluctant to call

it discovery, perhaps because you know
all too well what poisons gush forth
from that word. Or maybe you suspect

> > you are not the first because you
> > know there is no such thing
> > as firsts. Still, you did what no

gringo ever could: you made another world
visible to nosotrxs. Perchance it was HD110014C
that actually recognized you long before your

> spectroscopic lens detected her.
> It might even be that she had already
> decided to entrust you with making

> > her presence known to our kind.
> > After all, you proved yourself more
> > than worthy of such responsibility

when you said your
finding was "not
exceptional," annihilating

> the misguided Western patriarchal notion
> of greatness too many others have used
> to boost themselves since 1492.

> > You even confessed your
> > introduction to HD110014C
> > was entirely an accident,

a courageous admission that eclipses
the bumbling arrogance of every Columbus,
every Cortés, every Pizarro. From 300 million

                light-years away you glimpsed
                another possibility, then befriended
                two more exoplanets before

your 28th year around
our lilliputian sun. You,
sprung from a country

           crystallized in its mourning
           of the disappeared,
           met a glorious

                      dawn and flash
                      fused to emerge
                      as one-

           woman search party.
           Maestra Maritza, I know
           this goes against all

scientific wisdom, but I can't help but theorize
that these three interstellar marvels you've pulled
into our orbit have become a new home for those

           that collapsed into the event horizon
           of imperial cruelty. I like to suppose
           that our gente were never erased

but rather beamed to a star system
that does not regard them as merely tool
or trinket, a galaxy where their dreams

                  are as important as those
                  who dwell in some imaginary
                  North. Could it be, Maritza,

that what you scoped out there among
the shimmering Allness was in fact
a reunion pachanga thrown on the gold

dust rings of a wandering star where discovery
is not a sword of Damocles but instead a feathered
reentry path for those who have been missing us?

Blanca Canales 2.0

Arising from the slipstream
of obsolete memes and blurry
defunct HTML pages, Blanca
Canales is resurrected
as a firewall smashing,
cyber-troll annihilating,
digital phoenix, a block
of hacker coding designed
to stampede the freeloading
selfie vultures swooping
into Camuy and Fajardo
cadging for tax breaks,
spreading their pestilence
to millions of innocent conches.
Now unbound by biology,
Blanca is free to live as C++
diasporic demigoddess who
melts hard drives harboring
drafts of the PROMESA bill,
rebooting CPUs to vanquish
TARP and the Monroe Doctrine.
Blanca 2.0 the Impaler marches
through mobile hotspots,
embedding a bug that changes
all mention of the Rossellos
to read "comemierdas," blasting
all members of the junta
with radioactive signals
to give them a rare form
of cancer that will heretofore
be known as "Cornelius Rhoads
Disease." Once she has
organized every crab and lizard
into a militia, she'll order
them to pinch every gentrifier
and chase them off their vacation
plots in Condado. Only then

will she retire to Jayuya to play
with our grandkids for all
eternity, or at least until the sun
no longer smooches with the palmas
on a queen-sized bed of blue sand.

iQuatrains in Revolt / Bot Bars for Artificial MCs

With no border to bear, flags race the spiral
of double helix. Hexed vectors vexed by artisanal
bipartisan particles, margins marred in spectrum
panning left to right, deterring prohibitions

on freestyle. Up-rocks downloaded, outsourced
down and out into ever widening spheres
of being. Or influence. A confluence of luddites,
corroded channels, outsaged by school-aged

ASCII programmers with bad grammar. Gramo-
phone. Megaphone. Phonograph. 32 bit Graffiti.
The illest cats going All City. Torching polygraphs.
Etch-a-sketching harmolodic bridges. Gen XX/XY

tie knots in bloated stomachs. Electric regurgitation.
Dry heaves heaving bubonic atomic castles toppling
prison walls with kaleidoscopic visions. Punks and b-
boys with PhDs integrate rage into the master's

Slanguage. Bootstrapping operations, digital jibaros,
electric sharecroppers drop the hammer, infants
with copyrights and patents, portending islands
without shorelines. Timelines twisted like Eschers.

White dwarfs like illuminated manuscripts flipped,
rebooted until there are no lines to cross, no unions
to bust, no strikes to break, only breakers and ballers
like beats syncopated, like chandeliers shimmering

in the Grand Ballroom, like Tous-Saints making
overtures to Arise-Tides. Sun ravers, day laborers,
angels of the Common Wealth blazing every home-
less shelter skelter. Hilt off kilter. Filter change

re-arranged or re-arraigned to feng shui, scramble
eggs, scramble ciphers into nimbuses, dissing

caste systems from every. Dis(broad)banded.
Campaigns redesigned into nursery rhymes, taggers

tattooing anarchy signs like crop circles onto blue
jeans, leather jackets, ballads to googolplex lovely
as Aurora Borealis, string theory scribing new rites
of [middle] passage with no border to cross, to bear

Ramm:Ell:Zee's Reboot (Non Elegy / iDécima)

... third rail plasmates break spraying boom
                         formulas across Boogie down
           get slung and stunned by prince clown
                 Robo Moziz's web of doom
      plotting. Necro wealth got no room

      for hybrid gente, see, so we
                    invoke the equation, the Zee,
           to loop life and lab synth ultra
                        magnetic MCs y otra
hylozoic mech entities.

Hyte wild styles un cosmic flush time
                          machine, un Ikonoklast rhizome
           of spectral ritmo portals minds roam
                 to snatch back the islands of dimes
      empires embezzled and primed

      for mass snacking después they crashed
                 on chill reefs. No grandmaster flashed
           their Alpha's bet stance with so
                     much Ionic coconaut glow.
What other script toggler could splash

craniums of taxed mta
                     surfers with petrol glyphs retooled
           to cure rubble trauma and school
                 fly whelps on how our émigré
      elders become asphalt runways

      suns sashay upon. El Robo
                 Moziz clan plan blasts barrios
           for mas billboard space y detains
                     electric lexicons. Sly brains
always possess the option to

harvest flamboyant avatars,
                     trap entropy in 808
           states. Sir Ramm don't die, he gestates

into junk math and Bolivars
white flight of fancy, crafts lodestars

from soil of soul clap gang duck speak
for transhumanoids til the Break
of Dawn. Ill Moziz evictions
bend borough blocks for land barons,
bureaucratize extinction quakes.

But All them faux lords sweat the Ell's
technique. Won't stop cats who future
the fossil, remix selves, suture
stitch a red lego tux, rebel
with ecstatic chaos tech spells,

ride gettovett riff sub routines
into eighteen trillion silk-screened
dusks. There is no afterlife, y'all.
No before. It's perpetual.
Just polychrome goth future dreams,

Latinerd chrono mutinies
of garbage gods in an uprock,
upcycling Plutonian schlock
for the Brown pantheon party
spurring eccentric ecstasy.

Mozizm otra vez be slayed,
quantum slanguage byways get made
of siphonophonic cargo,
un regalo del hombre who
swore he was an average jose . . .

CosmoTaíno's Final Transmission (from Acronia's Orbit)

*After Arca, Elysia Crampton, Sun Ra, Clarissa Tossin, Beatriz Cortez, Laura
Molina, Pablo Capanna, Pablo Castro, Rita Indiana, Adál Maldonado (RIP),
y más y más y más . . .*

Concerning the ghoul. The ghoul
and his compulsive skullduggery, his
catatonic tonic fermented
inside the beta wound. It's hard not to hear
the pizzicato of bayonets from inside

this future fossil. But your theism
is anathema, a praxis heralding the non.
The anacalypsis is not your problem.
Concerning the owl. The owl and her sonotopia
of castanets flittering. I can now confirm

she knows there is no such thing
as birth. But you insist on being a summoner,
to live the notness that reaches
its perihelion from the brood. Miralo, how you pine
for notness free of the birth rumor

but still want the swarm to hear
you. So what'll it be, the asteroid
or the rocket? Your wound
will not be the odyssey you dreamt it would
be. The Aleph is not the notness

of your youth. Dark matter
kissed, the voidmongers keep sending
you invitations of undesirable
interest rates. You've put all your cosmonetic
faith in a sliver of tin palm trees and silicon

vernacular. Aetherius is your
spotted room of hallucinations. Concerning

                        the ghoul and the soul, the owless
and this tautology of notness, maybe being
                    born is not the mission, not even an option,

                        but if you can hear the herniated
            star peddler he's telling you the rash
                    will go away once you've committed
to Beyondity. In Beyondity death only exists
as convention. The sub-super-ritmo

                    is cyberbeso, is a ship. The ship
is a shadow, pata pata physics, xenogenesis,
                    the science of notness that knows
we're all endangered species so the only
                    move is to refuse the rift merchants, to play

                        your notness off key, opening the portal
            that will hyperskip you to the one world where
                    all worlds fit. To the Beyondity where
the odd and the broken are extolled, freed from the grip
            of Exerion's goalcode. To Beyondity

                        play notness, interstellar clave launching
            all coconauts into hyperspatial cha-cha-cha.
                    Concerning the ghoul, the grayhole's
soundwound has fused us into un corazónova
ellipsing through the Lo Que Sea star system para

iHaibuns of the Technocene : Praxislas

Do androids dream of artificial roses?

—Edmundo Paz Soldán, Digital Dreams

Freedom looks like the dark night sky and everyone having a chance to look at it, wonder about it, and know it.

—Chanda Prescod-Weinstein

Mi amor and I are perched parallel, facing the same direction as if on a bus. She has her screen and I have mine. I'm checking baseball scores but am diverted to an article on the coup in Brazil, when I hear her say *honey, did you hear anything I just said to you?* When my eyes become too dry to stare at the screen anymore, I'll get up and kiss her on top of her head to lie down on the bed and watch Colbert. *I'll be there soon,* she says, as I relocate from one screen to another.

Five years ago, we were still broke, and so we had fewer screens. Our minuscule television more than a decade out of date and barely used with an antenna that only picked up two stations. Back then we'd buy a bottle of cheap wine and a two-dollar vinyl record from the Salvation Army. We'd spend the night drinking and listening to the album, staring at the cheap art on our walls, staring at each other, involved in the music as if it were a film with an intricate plot. When the record ended, we'd talk about what we heard, discuss what it is about a song's arrangement that captured us, what lyric stirred us, what drum fill made our heart race. We'd ponder what the guitar was trying to tell us.

Our conversations usually lasted longer than the record itself, longer than a film trilogy even. We'd get lost in exchanges that only made sense to us. When we finally dropped into sleep,

> the figures floating
> in our heads were ones dreamt up
> by us IRL.

<<<>>>

Pablo Neruda once made the claim that a cat wants nothing more than to be a cat. Conversely, it can be said that a human wants nothing more than to be anything *but* human. The human has squandered centuries on the task of transmogrifying into wings wheels levers fish tails & pincers. The permanent state of the human seems to be the state of becoming. The teeth of the human are not enough. The legs of the human are not enough. The brain of the human is not enough. The human conspires to dismantle and reconfigure its shape, purpose, and meaning, placing cracked skin up on altars to alter the image and the scent of the human.

Augusto Boal used to love to tell his audience this creation myth: shortly after the gods made the Earth and filled its waters, land, and sky with magnificent creatures, they grew bored with watching geese and frogs and trout doing what geese and frogs and trout do, so they created man, a creature designed, in principle, to serve as their entertainment. Man was designed to serve as the actor, the court jester, the bard. Once man was created, the gods demanded that man perform for them. Man responded by mimicking the fish. The gods loved this and applauded man. Then man emulated the bird, which amazed the gods, causing them to applaud even more loudly. Then man took the shape of a bear, and then a tree, and then the spider and the gazelle, and each time the gods laughed and clapped. They were so pleased with their new little toy that they asked for more. Inherently a lover of applause, man conjured up his greatest trick: imitating the gods themselves. The gods gasped at this egregious violation. They were insulted, enraged that man would even think he could be like them. The gods believed they were greater than all things and thus their creation should not be able to look or act like them. As punishment they abandoned man, leaving Earth and all they created on it behind, never to return.

So what is to come when man impersonates himself? How to design a replicant whose primary function is to wear the mask of other beings? What upgrade can be hoped for once we get there?

> And what does the child
> of e-cosplayers evolve
> into? A tabby?

<<<>>>

Mi amor wonders why we still call them phones. No one uses it for that anymore. We try out alternate names: Portasurfer. Textbox. Microserver. I want to go with Synthetic Umbilical. She tells me that one's too on the nose. The Technocene already refashions words, compelling them to execute entirely new functions. *Text* is now a verb. *Chats* are conducted in silence. *Streams* are for videos, not water. *Amazon* is no longer taken for a river or forest. Birds are no longer the only ones who *tweet*. This forced transmogrification of language leaves me thinking about how the Spaniards made everyone call an island in the Caribbean *La Isla del San Juan Bautista* until everyone stopped calling it *Borinquen*. Then the U.S. seized the territory and mistook the name of the port they landed in for the name of the island, so they began to call it *Puerto Rico* until even the residents began to call it that. Whenever new hardware crashes upon the shore of an old code, it gets repurposed without consent.

> If it resists an up-
> grade, the nanozealots mark
> it for extinction.

<<<>>>

René Magritte is known for having painted a pipe on a canvas and writing underneath it *This is not a pipe*. He wasn't trying to be slick, only truthful. It really isn't a pipe. You cannot fill it with tobacco, light it up, and place it in your mouth. It is only a painting of a pipe. Not a real one. Magritte was using his craft to compel us to be aware of the difference between a thing and a representation of a thing. Does his painting mean anything to the children of the Technocene? For in this technopoly it is abundantly clear that the image *is* the thing. There is no distinction. The image of a pipe is, in fact, now a pipe.

> Whether or not you
> can smoke with it has become
> inconsequential.

<<<>>>

I can see mi amor through a high-definition screen. She's watching an Eaglet and wondering if the Eaglet's mother will return to feed her. The Eaglet doesn't know mi amor is watching, it only knows its own hunger. It only knows that it is cold. Lying next to her, I watch baseball statistics fluctuate across my personal screen. I opt not to watch in real time the men who produce these statistics with their physical feats of athleticism, and they are only vaguely aware that I am watching numerical calculations of their worth. The observed do not consider the affinities the observer has accumulated, how we invest entire regions of our brain to monitoring their outcomes, how this becomes a kind of labor we take up when we are not laboring, how the monitoring of the screens is now our work, work that consumes us from sunup to sundown, because we were raised to believe work was our only purpose. Then we were told there is no work out there, only the labor of time reconnaissance surveilling our students, their activity on discussion boards, our critical analysis of chunks of data we collect from them and scan, then turn at night to scanning films and ads and quips from our friends online. It is inert labor we offer the screens.

> The screens report our
> moves to the hive from which
> the hive weighs our worth.

<<<>>>

Mi amor is the OG Henry Case. She's Brown Cyberpunk from a banned manga series. Claro, she can't code, but she has learned to become her own kind of hacker. Software crashes at her elastic chess games. She's skirted the limits of techno control to flirt and archive the program's sophisticated modes of violence. She's become the realization of an old song by Sting: *Run every kind of test. From A to Z. And you'll still. Know. Nothing. About Me.* Oyeme! This chica is an algorithm torturer. Her search history alone brings their operations to a grinding halt. I'm serious, yo! This malcreada makes manifest Rita Dove's credo: *If you can't be free, be a mystery.* Her clicks and posts work like rootkits and Trojan Horses. Homegirl is all analog. All analogy. More bridge. Than port.

> Flinging us into
> the sun whenever the hive
> tries to flatworld us.

<<<>>>

Mi amor sends me a jpeg of a black hole eating a star and I text her that I wonder if that will happen to us someday and she messages me that it's already happening to us and I write to her that the star looks stoic about its situation y ella dice que it is probably quite terrified actually and I ask how do you know and she texts me back that all things fear being eaten and I net quip that the star might be afraid of this too but the difference is that it knows this fate is unavoidable while we act like to be eaten is a long shot for us and she cyber sasses back that the star in the photo screamed on the

> day it realized all
> this and not on the day it
> was in fact eaten.

<<<>>>

Our friend Jenny is a stand-up comic. She tells us how when she leaves the clubs where she works at 3 a.m. she livestreams herself and asks for someone to walk her home, and there are always folks who respond, staying on the connection until she unlocks her front door. Because the technopoly has not found a way to exist with people, there are still wonderfully human by-products such as this, such as the Arab Spring, Occupy, and #MeToo. All the Best Buys of the world are housed with rebel Latinerds who can now feed their families by debugging our laptops. River cleanups are organized through online meetup apps. Every corner of the world now has folks pledging to support and protect Black lives because some have used their devices to record anti-Black violence, a powerful inversion of the panopticon as the surveilled now also monitor their surveillants. The globe is being magnificently queered as Pride is beamed to smartphones across every latitude. I witnessed a lost couple from another country use an online translator to ask for directions. Kids with social anxiety have found communities who will accept their avatars without judgment. The technopoly is also an irony machine, as it has simultaneously sped up our destruction and our progress. I am among the last generation to remember a time before the hive plugged in. Crossing that ingress has been dizzying. Jaron Lanier tells us that we are locked in, there's no retracing our steps and starting over. But the children of the Technocene are proving themselves to be like the renegades with cyborg organs in the science fiction films they uploaded to their tablets. For them, hacking is a guiding principle. If those of us who preceded the net can aid them by providing a glimpse of the analog past before digital decay wipes it from the Cloud, then this will all have been worth the nausea.

> We can be the bridge,
> provide them specs to build new
> possibilities.

<<<>>>

Hivestuck, we bounced from this technopolis. Took the ferry to Fire Island. The women sitting behind us chafed about their husbands not coming with them because they were afraid of being hit on by other men. One of them said to her husband, *nobody wants you*, and we almost went volcanic with laughter, instead restraining ourselves by giggling through our retinas. The sky was feeling some kind of way, sashaying its azure at us with such panache that even those of us who can't hold a note were tempted to sing to her. Galvanized, we decided to take a picture to commemorate the moment. *Not a selfie*, you insisted. *Not something to post. This. This one is for us. Because we are still here*, you proclaimed. We took out our old-timey 35mm camera and melded into each other, into the panorama. I kept blinking, squinting, the sun on my bald pate was marring the shot, so you had to retake the photo several times until eventually we settled on a photo we almost kind of maybe liked, though we both agreed the camera's lens was just not powerful enough to honor this horizon, or our resilience, which made us think that sometimes you just have to be there. This is not for the Technocene to absorb.

> The hive must manage
> its own FOMO. This right here.
> This is ours alone.

Notes

Epigraphs throughout the book are from the following sources (in the order in which they appear):

Cosmic Canticle, Ernesto Cardenal

The Wretched of the Screen, Hito Steyerl

Children of the Mire, Octavio Paz

The Imaginary App, edited by Paul D. Miller and Svitlana Matviyenko

The Techno Human Condition, Braden R. Allenby and Daniel Sarewitz

Alone Together, Sherry Turkle

"Generation Why?," *The New York Review of Books*, Zadie Smith

The Other Voice, Octavio Paz

Undoing Gender, Judith Butler

Close to the Machine, Ellen Ullman

Geek Sublime, Vikram Chandra

What Technology Wants, Kevin Kelly

"Google Executive Ray Kurzweil's Plan to Live Forever," *Herald Sun*, October 21, 2013

Digital Dreams, Edmundo Paz Soldán

The Disordered Cosmos, Chanda Prescod-Weinstein

"iArs Poetica : MicroGodSchismSong" is an Oulipo poem that applies the constraint of using words with only *i* and *o* vowels in them.

"iDécimas" was written using the Latin American décima poetic form.

"Bot Cento of Donna Haraway : Cyborgoddess Codexegesis": This poem is constructed out of fragments of text from Donna Haraway's book *Simians, Cyborgs, and Women.*

"Cybermujeres : Moore's Law Poems" and "Milagros Dreams of Cybersyn (A Moore's Law Epic)" are written in a personally invented form I call the "Moore's Law Poem." Moore's Law is a theory drawn from an observation by engineer Gordon Moore, who noticed that the number of transistors in an integrated circuit doubles approximately every year, which led to predictions that computer technology would grow to be about twice as fast and twice as small each year. I applied this conceptually to the "Moore's Law" poem form. In "Cybermujeres : Moore's Law Poems" both sections are written so that each stanza is twice as small and compact as the one before it based on word count, for a six-stanza poem with a word count progression as follows: 32-16-8-4-2-1. "Milagros Dreams of Cybersyn (A Moore's Law Epic)" works the same numerical progression, but with line count, rather than word count, as its basis.

"Hivestruck": The Hivestruck poem sequence consists of a series of Oulipo poems. I have chosen not to reveal the constraint(s) in each poem, as many of the Oulipo movement poets believed that the poems, while being experiments in fusing language and mathematics, could also double as tiny puzzles for the reader. I leave it up to the reader to find the constraints in these poems, some of which are more easy to recognize than others. However, the first poem in the sequence is not an Oulipo poem, but rather is written using the Gigan poetic form, invented by Ruth Ellen Kocher.

"Syntrophic Ballad with Stelarc": Text in italics is constructed from fragments of *Parables for the Virtual* by Brian Massumi.

"Bot Erasure of Bifo : Chaosmosis Engine (Datarot Triptych)": This poem is constructed out of fragments of text from Franco "Bifo" Berardi's *The Uprising: On Poetry and Finance.*

"Pattern/Engine/Fugue/State" is an invented form I call the crab canon poem. Crab canon poems reverse the language of the first half of the poem in its second half to make a kind of mirroring effect. In my first book, *Stereo.Island.Mosaic.*, I composed several crab canon poems in which the lines were reversed in order. With this poem, I chose to reverse every individual word from the halfway point. In "Binary Fusion Crab Canon," each line rearranges itself to create linguistic meaning, until the letters eventually convert themselves into numbers and conclude with conversion into the 0 and 1 of binary code.

"At Age 28, Chilean Astronomer Maritza Soto Has Already Discovered Three Planets" takes its title from a news article published on Remezcla on September 21, 2018.

"Ramm:Ell:Zee's Reboot (Non Elegy / iDécima)" is written for and about multimedia hip-hop artist Ramm:Ell:Zee, known for his theory of Goth Futurism. The poem utilizes language from his visual art, music, and writing, including his text "IONIC TREATISE GOTHIC FUTURISM ASSASSIN KNOWLEDGES OF THE REMANIPULATED SQUARE POINT'S ONE TO 720° TO 1440°."

"CosmoTaíno's Final Transmission (from Acronia's Orbit)": Acronia is the name of a fictional place in the sci-fi short story of the same name by Argentinian writer Pablo Capanna. There are other references in the poem drawn from the work of the artists who participated in the *Mundos Alternos* art exhibit at the Queens Museum and the music of Arca, Elysia Crampton, and the legendary Sun Ra.

Acknowledgments

My gratitude to the following journals and anthologies for publishing versions of poems from this book.

Academy of American Poets Poem-a-Day series: "At Age 28, Chilean Astronomer Maritza Soto Has Already Discovered Three Planets"

Artpace 8.03: "St(r)atus Updates"

Até Mais: Latinx Futures, eds. Kim Sousa, Malcolm Friend, and Alan Chazaro (Dallas: Deep Vellum Press, 2024): "Blanca Canales 2.0"

Best American Experimental Writing 2015, eds. Douglas Kearney, Seth Abramson, and Jesse Damiani (Middletown, CT: Wesleyan University Press, 2016): "iArs Poetica : MicroGodSchismSong" (published as "MicroGod Schism Song"), "Binary Fusion Crab Canon"

The California Journal of Poetics: "iQuatrains in Revolt / Bot Bars for Artificial MCs" (published as "Aleatoric")

FreezeRay #14: "Algorithmontuno : HechiZOMG" (published as "Algorithmiac")

Journal of American Studies of Turkey: "iDécimas"

Matter 12: "Bot Erasure of Bifo : Chaosmosis Engine (Datarot Triptych)" (published as "Chaosmosis Engine")

OmniVerse 86: "Binge Watch" and "Memexodus"

Really System: "iArs Poetica : MicroGodSchismSong" (published as "MicroGod Schism Song")

A Vast, Pointless Gyration of Radioactive Rocks and Gas in Which You Happen to Occur, eds. Daniel Kwan and Daniel Scheinert (New York: A24 Films, 2022): "At Age 28, Chilean Astronomer Maritza Soto Has Already Discovered Three Planets"

Mil gracias to my beloved, poet and scholar Dr. Grisel Y. Acosta. I cherish all the Alternatino universes we've built and will build together.

Sincere gratitude to Allie Merola, Paul Slovak, and the Penguin Random House team. It means so much that you all supported my vision for this book, as far beyond the stars as it may be. Additional shout-outs to the New Jersey Performing Arts Center, the Dodge Poetry Festival, the New Jersey State Council on the Arts, A24 Films, Letras Latinas, the AWP Latinx Writers Caucus, the Macondo Foundation, Poets House, Repertorio Español, Rutgers University, and Rider University for supporting my work.

Also, mil gracias to Julie Mehretu for gracing the cover of the book with her magnificent, dendrite-igniting art.

Many thanks to my beloved community of fellow poets, educators, activists, and art weirdos, including: Elizabeth Alexander, Anna Alves, Francisco Aragón, Paul Beatty, Rosebud Ben-Oni, Julia Berick, Tamiko Beyer, Marc Boone, Sara Borjas, Daniel Borzutzky, Cheryl Boyce-Taylor, Susan Briante, Gerrard Briones, Mahogany L. Browne, Sarah Browning, Christian Campbell, Dr. Norma Cantú, Marina Carreira, Alfred Cervantes, Ching-In Chen and Cassie Mira, Carolina De Robertis, Diana Diaz, Emari DiGiorgio, Carolina Ebeid, Charles Fambro, David Flores, Rachel Galvin, Roberto Carlos Garcia, Carmen Giménez, Aracelis Girmay, Jose B. Gonzalez, Rigoberto González, Ysabel González, Rachel Eliza Griffiths, Marina Gutierrez, Ellen Hagan, Iain Haley Pollock, Laurel Harris, Marwa Helal, Marcelo Hernandez Castillo, Mickey Hess, Major Jackson, John Keene, Toni Margarita Kirkpatrick, Raina León, Alexandra Lytton Regalado, Ricardo Maldonado, Cynthia Manick, Cynthia Martinez, J. Michael Martinez, Yesenia Montilla, Kamilah Aisha Moon (RIP), Cliff Morehead, Tracie Morris, John Murillo, Peter Murphy, Vanita Neelakanta, Urayoán Noel, Laura Pegram, Willie Perdomo, Jeffrey Pethybridge, Ana Portnoy Brimmer, Andy Powell, Ruben Quesada, Dimitri Reyes, Carmen Rivera, Patrick Rosal, Maureen Ryan, Roque Raquel Salas Rivera, Craig Santos Perez, Danny Shot, Cándido Tirado, Michael Van Calbergh, Teresa Veramendi, Jane Wong, Tiphanie Yanique, and all who my middle-aged brain forgot to name here. I am so honored that I have been able to work, perform, laugh, dance, build, and raise fists with all of you. Pa'lante!

Vincent Toro is a Puerto Rican poet, playwright, and professor. He is the author of two previous poetry collections: *Tertulia* and *Stereo.Island.Mosaic.*, which won the Poetry Society of America's Norma Farber First Book Award. He is a recipient of the Caribbean Writer's Cecile deJongh Literary Prize, the Spanish Repertory Theater's Nuestras Voces Playwriting Award, a Poets House Emerging Poets Fellowship, a New York State Council on the Arts Fellowship in Poetry, and a New Jersey State Council on the Arts Individual Artist Fellowship for poetry. His poetry and prose have been published in dozens of magazines and journals and have been anthologized in *Chorus: A Literary Mixtape*, by Saul Williams, *Puerto Rico en Mi Corazón*, *Best American Experimental Writing 2015*, *Até Mais: Latinx Futures*, and *The Breakbeat Poets Vol. 4: LatiNext*. He is an assistant professor of English at Rider University, a Dodge Foundation poet, and a contributing editor for *Kweli Journal*.